VE – Poetry

Marc Yeats

Collected Poems
Volume 1

Vision Edition

Vision Edition
www.visionedition.com

Vision Edition 027-TP

ISBN 978-1-0687122-0-3

Photo by Lucas Yeats

CONTENTS

From Music, Painting, Landscape and Me
August 2023-January 2024

PREFACE

"Painting is a form of poetry, colours are words, their relations rhythms, the completed painting a completed poem."[1]

I am not alone as I write—several of Marc's artworks are on the walls, sumptuous, dark, playful, delicate abstract depictions of the landscapes that he loves so much and there are musical scores on the table next to me, riots and clouds of painterly gestures which accumulate and dissolve across the pages. Marc's music is in my ears, its complexity and fantastic wildness both confounding and exciting. The space is filled with his virtuosic, deeply personal and truly remarkable creations, and now, there is a volume of poetry. I could not be more honoured to be composing this preface for a friend who has been described by Peter Maxwell Davies as "breathtakingly original", and by Stephen Davismoon as "one of the most prolific and influential composers and creative artists of his generation in the UK."

I met Marc for the first time in 2015 in a tiny café, The Horse with the Red Umbrella in Dorchester (England) and was bowled over by the immensity of his energy, indeed walking away a little overwhelmed. I am still overwhelmed by this energy, understanding it now as an insatiable, yes, obsessive drive to explore and share his perception of the world through such a multiplicity of expressive means. Marc's own book *Music, Painting, Landscape and Me* considers these means in a tour de force of intellectual exploration into the multifaceted relationships that inform his artistic and compositional practice, with a small number of contemplative but incisive poems illuminating the text—intimate, even fragile perhaps within the surrounding philosophical landscape. The structural interpolation of these tiny, related poetic moments draws the

---

[1] Quotation attributed to Sonia Delaunay in Cohne, Arthur Allen, *Sonia Delaunay: Life of an Artist*, H. N. Abrams, 1975, p. 28.

xi

reader's focus in and out of the densely layered sweep of theoretical discussion in a way that can be likened to Marc's approach to composition, where he talks of "polarised intensities, contextual, temporal ambiguities and perceptual polytemporal relationships", all aspects that can as easily be relatable to his painting. Marc has an innate understanding of how literary, aural and tactile material functions at so many levels, from ravishing surface coruscation to deep-level structure with its constantly transforming perspectives, both temporal and textural. These are languages that shift and swirl, that ground and elevate us with such intensity and clarity of purpose.

But what of this new volume of poems? Although undoubtedly enriched by knowing Marc's music and artworks, the poems can be enjoyed thoroughly without any knowledge of him as an internationally performed composer, most recently by the BBC Scottish Symphony Orchestra (*the unimportance of events* (2021) and *a point in the landscape* (2020) for Tectonics Glasgow 2021 and 2024 respectively) or as an acclaimed artist represented by The John Davies Gallery.

Marc's poetry is a perfect manifestation of Plato's statement *"Thinking is the talking of the soul with itself."* The poems are his 'thinking out loud', allowing us glimpses into a mind that is rigorously questioning, observing, deconstructing and recreating his own inner world whilst also exploring the beauty and visceral drama of the outer world with an almost Romantic sensibility. Although there is a perceivable change in language between the more overtly luminous works of 2005 written on Skye and those composed in 2023-4 following the period of Marc's academic research for his doctorate and ensuing book, several themes are revisited across the two periods. There are multi-perspective preoccupations with the ephemerality and heaviness of time (*seeing backwards/looking shouldn't numb me/Long Covert*), the search for self as an artist and man (*here/without touching it/when walking/who am I kidding?/I won't be corralled*), a fascination with the unseen, the imagined (*presence is where?/is thinking art?/asleep*), with process (*words/meanings are embedded*), with sex and the physical body (*rutting is real/it's difficult to know/Knockholt*), with human relationships (*I know what's said/if I do not look/in the rain*) and interrogations into the interplay between music and painting (*where?/what I am there/traces the composer leaves behind*) often articulated through detailed observations of the walked landscape (*listening landscapes noise/being here looking/it's difficult to know/I am not the land*). Whilst on the surface some poems have the transparency of watercolour (*we haunt the light/in shadow*), and others the quality of heavy, layered oils (*how conceiving/variable fields*), the intense beauty and directness of Marc's poetic language unifies them. These are poems which invite us to accompany Marc on walks across chalk downland and hillsides, to converse about everything that makes the world, and him, so extraordinary.

Sadie Harrison
Shaftesbury, June 2024

INTRODUCTION

Writing poetry has been an erratic affair for me. Beyond my scattered early experiments, there have been only two significant periods of poetic activity: during November 2005, a time marked by turmoil, when I penned a slew of poems mirroring existential, philosophical and personal dilemmas, and from August 2023 to February 2024 following the completion of my book, *Music, Painting, Landscape and Me.*[2] These periods of creativity have culminated in the collection present in this volume. Outside these bursts of activity, there was silence. This intermittent writing pattern leads me to wrestle with identifying as a poet. I imagine that poets engage with their craft daily, much like the consistency I apply to composing music and painting. It seems incongruous that a 'real' poet would allow an eighteen-year hiatus between periods of creativity. Yet, pragmatism suggests that if one's intent is to write poetry, and this endeavour results in creations recognised as poetry by readers, then the title of being a poet is earned, regardless of any concerns about irregularity in output. Now, in 2024, with over two hundred and thirty poems presented here, I finally embrace the label of a poet, adding it to my identities alongside painter, composer, practice researcher and writer as work that extends the interpretive possibilities for my creative activities.

Extending interpretive possibilities was a prime consideration when I recognised the power of poetry to convey additional meaningfulness through the written word. This insight led me to incorporate several of my 2005 poems within *Music, Painting, Landscape and Me*. In the book, I embarked on an introspective journey, weaving together the symbolic realms of music and painting through the written word. This endeavour expanded upon the immediacy of engagement with my compositions and paintings and what those artworks 'say', offering further

---

[2] Yeats, Marc, *Music, Painting, Landscape and Me*, Vision Edition, 2024.

understanding and dialogue concerning their interrelation and connection to the landscape. In the first chapter of the book, titled *The List*, I explain that poetry offered

"an alternative way to express ideas I find difficult to capture using regular syntax, offering both open and closed propositions to reflect the complexities of experience. The poems show my preoccupation with many of the issues highlighted in Music, Painting, Landscape and Me, stretching back across decades, some to childhood. The poems use vague language to hint at things, allude to, and look indirectly upon issues of time, permanence, flux, and a whole gamut of 'lived experiences'."[3]

With the poems integrated, the manuscript of the book was finalised. I shared it with several individuals for feedback. One of them, my friend Carmel Gardner, was captivated by the book, particularly the included poems, and shared how they affected her. Carmel proposed that I publish the poems alongside any additional ones I had, creating a collected volume. Over the subsequent weeks, Carmel's suggestion resonated with me deeply. I returned to the poems I had written in 2005 and, thinking carefully about them, realised that not all of those poems stood the test of time, that I had selected the best of the collection relevant for inclusion in my book (several 2005 poems were excluded due to their deeply personal and emotionally charged content—modes of expression that would have felt out of place in that publication), and that although thematically consistent with much of my current thinking, those verses were written in a former voice.

Including the originally excluded poems plus a small number that had been restructured for inclusion in this volume, I realised there were still too few verses in the 2005 series to make a satisfying collection. Uncertain how to proceed, I remembered

---

[3] Yeats, p. 10.

an idea that occurred to me while writing *Music, Painting, Landscape and Me* to re-present concepts of the book using only the flexibility and flux of poetic language to express my thoughts and, moving beyond that, verses sharing the emotional conditions experienced as an artist and composer—perspectives I had largely excluded from the book. Being an advocate of self-borrowing, transformation and the repurposing of creative materials, processes I use frequently in music composition and painting, I saw these poems as a possibility to 'transduce' my research-based writing from one field of expression to another, exponentially increasing its potential for meaningfulness beyond its original incarnation. This 'transduction' meant that the writing in *Music, Painting, Landscape and Me* would permeate much of the poetry assembled in this collection and that despite the surface differences between the two, the nature of these books would be profoundly bound together by the 'genetic' thread of my creative practice and 'lived experiences' as an artist. Moving forwards, I considered the 2005 poems as foundational works, serving as both context and bedrock for all subsequent poems.

Between August 2023 and January 2024, and knowing how to proceed, I wrote poems almost daily, sometimes several each day. These works are laid out chronologically as a sequential and sometimes non-sequential exploration of the subject areas within *Music, Painting, Landscape and Me*. Accordingly, the organisation of this poetry collection offers a clear division between the 2005 writings and the more numerous later works. Some poems are aphoristic, perhaps no more than a few words, while others are relatively extended. Their language ranges from clear to paradoxical, enigmatic, dense and opaque, reflecting the indeterminacies and contradictions of my thought. As well as presenting ideas around the why and how of life, I also ventured into the new territory of expressing feelings relating to the acts of making paintings, writing and music compositions, along with reactions describing the personal impacts of being an artist, all tempered by whatever was going on in my emotional world at the time of writing. As such, the poems are coloured by opinions, experiences, memories, loss, locations, emotions, introspection, speculations, projection, description, confusion, sensation, yearning, unrest, memory, frustration and further questioning. Sometimes obsessive, many poems revisit similar territory, presenting those ideas from different perspectives to forge a better understanding of their content.

By the close of 2023, I had amassed a substantial collection of poems but needed clarification about what to do with them once written. At this time, *Music, Painting, Landscape and Me* was going through the final preparations for publication with Vision Edition, so it was a great surprise when, on New Year's Eve, I received an email from John Palmer, Vision Edition's director, with a proposal to publish the 2005 poems already in the book along with my newly written collection in a separate volume dedicated to my poetry. Overjoyed, I accepted the offer immediately.

Spurred on, I enthusiastically began writing the final group of poems (12th of January to the 23rd of February 2024) brought together under the title of *The Wenninger Letters* that are based wholly on aspects of correspondence between myself and Markus Wenninger. Markus, a multifaceted artist described on his Twitter profile as an enthusiast of flute, chirography, Feldenkrais, kinesthetics, yoga, pedagogy, neuroplasticity, snuff and skateboarding, was a companion throughout the writing of *The List*. Markus served as an invaluable sounding board through our ongoing correspondence. His insights into hermeneutics, interpretation and embodiment, along with introductions to concepts including PK Coupling and the philosophies of Jacques Derrida and Ernst Cassirer, significantly enriched my exploration of embodiment, communication and perception throughout the book. The poems comprising this final collection are responses and provocations to the many avenues of thought he opened in his letters to me. They are also profoundly concerned with issues central to that book.

By the end of February 2024, I felt I had completed my task, and this current period of writing poetry had concluded. I also achieved my goal of transforming the ideas present in *Music, Painting, Landscape and Me* from one species of writing to another, opening and exploring additional territory in the process. Looking back over this period of creativity, I am reminded that the impetus to write more poems came from the initial remarks Carmel made about my first book and the poems it held when reading the draft manuscript. Recognising the galvanising power of her words upon my own, I dedicate *Collected Poems Volume 1* to Carmel.

Marc Yeats
Crewkerne, June 2024

Skye-2005

we haunt the light
(Waternish, Isle of Skye, November 2005)

we haunt the light
where
in temporal fragility
it blossoms

music fixes

music fixes time and place in suspended animation
released only through its sonic key
to reconstitute the moment
instantly sweeping far to where it opens me
convoluting through to a new land
fully formed beyond words and mass
to pulsating energy, untouched and present
as a breathless moment of return

the edge

the edge is the place to be
from here
you can see what is
and what is to come
it is knowledge and potential
but the cost is high
when you burn brightly from both ends

fear defines us

fear defines us
specifies our borders
furnishes our state
holds us down
and blinds

a local map

a local map
in a foreign land
will free your hand
to forge a new route
and seek from outside
what is lost within

and when found
peak-fill the familiar
with joyous thoughts
to loosen out the fires
concealing darkness
in those narrow places

seeing backwards

seeing backwards
we move forwards
our past colouring futures
that trip us to fall
for in this moment
today's tomorrow
is already yesterday

minds pattern randomness

minds pattern randomness
but uncomfortable with chaos
we stop, hold, make solid
and crush wonder

threadbare map

threadbare map
I know so well
every crevice fingered
intricately travelled but still lost
on a journey
to nowhere in particular

this journey

this journey liberates us from artificial restrictions
from the brightness of our captivity
and any compulsion to inflate our significance
allowing a breaking of bonds
to reveal concealed illusions once held as fact
so we may confront the unsuspecting
with the truth of our new reality

here

here
from the highest point
I can see for miles

on a clear day
I can even see myself

though we mark it

though we mark it, cut it, count it
we are never fixed
in the continuum of experience
lies infinite space
without line, dimension or division
save our mutilations
to stop this riot
and hang on
for dear life is measured
by fear of passage
to the other side of time

in the rain

in the rain
I knew she was dying
we sheltered
carefully
silent
in a crevice in the cliff
looking out

touch who is leaving

touch who is leaving
feel what will pass
into dust and time
to claw back hours, days, years
passing through my grasp
with such ease
that in the chase
expire

permanence

permanence
is the shadow
cast
by the edifice of time

we march through time

we march through time
motionless
to the ends of the world and beyond
blind, deaf and dumb
impotent to find order, sense and definition
to know without wisdom
and control and suppress the dance of creation
in a box so small
even our limitations cannot define it

a moment

a moment cannot be suspended
from past and future
for it lies in the space between them
as the present is indivisible
its core infinite
like the centre point of time
through which we move

to comprehend

to comprehend
is to see the surface

to intuit
is to live the paradox
that drives existence
to its beginning

gentle, simple truth

gentle, simple truth
therein
is often more potent
than the conspiracy of intellect
to quantify our souls

we linger

we linger in the shadows
watching our lives unfold
silent in the cacophony of choice and consequence
our feet glued to the ground
as scenes shift and characters evolve
impotent
waiting for the final act
the curtain to fall
and exit to the bright air of certainty

I urge the moment forwards

I urge the moment forwards
for another
more valuable one
is waiting
like sand
to fall through my fingers

damaged goods

damaged goods are everywhere
bruised, softened, putrefying
oozing
so close and sticky that fungus spreads
fruiting a glorious head of poisonous colour

but that wasn't the cause

but that wasn't the cause
a sinister flowering ate her inside out
its diabolic mass spreading through greyness
deconsecrating
turning flesh to jelly from womb to liver
and within the blink of an eye
she was gone

I do not register easily

I do not register easily in a room full of flowers
my bloom is tightly closed with colours hidden
until the time to open
glorious, in confidence
my trade as angel made
for I am not what you see
and not what you think you are
through me

like a chameleon

like a chameleon
he transforms in the undergrowth
different every time
his skin absorbing
to become context
leaving no trace for me to hold on to
for I am just a colour
passing across his intricate surface

in the fervour

in the fervour of our enthusiasm
and drawn to the boundaries of existence
some clarity emerges as silence moves outward
extrapolated to show what we believe we know

still ignorant of our limitations
we forget that fear hides in uncertainty
causing purposefulness to fade
so much so that our hands become tied

in stasis
frightened and reluctant to act
we cannot see beyond ourselves
or find the courage to move into the light

in shadow

in shadow
I cannot call the sweet light of day

for he is shining on you

this impossible dream

this impossible dream
is absorbed light and time
a dullness of red
set within a passive mechanism
into which I empty thought

but outside here
hot ice extinguishes old fires
creating every trace from earth to air
so I may solidify elements with form
unravelling any possible reality
as a visible darkness
penetrating everything

electric sleep

electric sleep
statically charged
a circuit of repulsion
like a magnet's shared polarity
pushing away to the extremities
far, but not far enough
aware of each other
every movement and breath
lying cold, detached
prickling with a proximity unwed
without rest
drifting apart and out of orbit
to a stronger gravity
and another's bed

the quietest point

the quietest point
is just before the storm
when intoxicated by escape
the beast emerges

rutting is real

rutting is real
pure sensation
like the earth beneath my feet
under my fingernails or in my mouth
its taste
connected to spasm and flesh
pulsing with the rush of it
over and again
my blood tells me
this is aliveness
and the point of me
so I grasp at the next thrill
fully aware that jerking through life
is meaning enough
when empty

if I do not look

if I do not look
I will not see you

then

where will I be?

the plug's pulled

the plug's pulled
and limp with empty
my juice spills out
powerless and drained
I suffocate in the void

I know what's said

I know what's said but cannot hear
and see what's written but cannot read
to touch your heart, unable to feel
other than you through me

but that's not you at all

is it?

my scars burn

my scars burn brightly

when kissed by acid
they flower

in pumping insecurity

in pumping insecurity
this heat-fire burns from a blue flame
weak, with no shadow cast
that in air, morphs into water
but as a form without elements of light
remains dark in the echoes
placed where there's nothing to see
and everything to hear
all drowning
under the whispers of others

we weave our webs

we weave our webs
unravel our shadows
smoothed with caresses
thin and slick with kindness
reluctant to release what we hold

and in pulling close
shrink our integrity
until the darkness ignites
and in reaching far
inflate our scars
before the light pierces
our compulsion to ensnare

and in casting wide
burgeon our pride
before the fall knocks us
from our mesh of tangled lies
to knit another entrapment
in which to hide

hitherto

hitherto, all things were equal
now, in an instant
the rug's been pulled
the floor has gone
and we float above
boats without anchors
drifting
mindful of the treacherous landfalls ahead

we travel

we travel on each other's love
strange, wild adventures
territories unknown
sometimes lost
blind alleys or mazes bewilder
searching always for home

From Music, Painting, Landscape and Me
August 2023-January 2024

a joy of venturing
(Crewkerne, 19th August 2023)

a joy of venturing into other worlds
to respond as sounding
by and through itself without modelling and only flow
is often overlooked as abundance-reaping
that like play submerged into silence
is instead expressed as music

outpourings from a noisy brain

outpourings from a noisy brain
scatter vistas
to territories surrounding harder-to-define areas
where thinking goes once it has been thought
but peripheral and blurred
it is impossible to achieve clarity
when all things are in motion

how conceiving

how conceiving one without the other
would deny the identity and interrelation of both
as correlating sensing to movement
is to perceive feeling as sound
and when analysing the phenomena
the physical location reinforces how imagining
and where this happens
is unknown

it is sometimes possible for me to describe
but rather, it stems from a complex interplay

today

today, when composing
some excitements are more robust than others
but regardless of intensity
bodily sound sensations continually shape my writing
and tomorrow
remembering
chalk landscapes will evoke the warmest feelings

variable fields

variable fields never find resolution
when positioned entirely within a self-portrait
that holds fluid intensity and surrender

it is, if you like
where words are unnecessary between physicality, thought
and its embodiment
as their transmission influences
how surface patterning articulates them
into less clear realms of sensation

as a generative force, it triggers
sound, colour, texture, structure and my body
uniting, advancing through all spaces
and how between, unsurprisingly
has arisen a union marrying feeling to performance

without touching it
(20th August 2023)

without touching it
the question "why am I?"
shows all parts in intercession
perhaps also singularly
but when thinking about it
the discourse feels curious
and I move away

I hear clearly

I hear clearly
and while standing the offer
it opens gradually
but I must not look too closely
or else it shifts again

travelling this path

travelling this path
I gather a lifetime's residue that holds fast
when mapping transforms into becoming
because the act of self-building is a tender affair

it shows capacity
as painter-conscious words signify making
to drive, define and articulate to expand
where experiences populate fragments
with connection and disconnection
and sometimes capricious
reflects this complexity to touch
and assemble understanding

where?

where is the overlap between us?

it is often iterative
as many things, not least meaningfulness
but music, painting, sculpture, word and dance
show the artist's ability to transmit
however arbitrarily
owing to communication being an agreement
disrupting affective properties as fixed conditions
where when in motion
certainty is detrimental to its value
and drifting what is thought specific
of notions and how much is known
with imbued and unspoken qualities
largely comprising of guesswork
seldom means anything at all

these pieces are scattered

these pieces are scattered
nevertheless, part of their image remains clear
here and there
and opening onto the subsequent
many of the fragments show dissipated propositions
and are constantly adaptive

this puzzle

this puzzle is emptiness
having the potential
to destabilise the former from view absolutely
as pieces are lost
it shows certitude in extrapolating its contribution
as the missing middle

missing
and without content, I defer
and fill the void
over and again
and here and there
destabilise it further

an upbeat

an upbeat
returning to locus without singular vision
it expands through spasm
of independent ranges, insights, possibilities
and curiosities within its flow
defined by its capacity to create anew
and open-ended to before shows its hand

can in questions, in questions following
or questions reflecting?

it is potential but not conclusion
the fact of the while within and outside
by utterances and passing thoughts

what I am there
(21st August 2023)

what I am there paints place-music
and writing, observing and about the activity
when thinking engages an aural-like quality
and looking positions the world as sound

how, as from myself

how, as from myself
meaning like music
remains through and about
a residue or trace?

listening landscapes noise

listening landscapes noise into form
and through paint and sound
as ways of sensing where across immanent milieus
expression shows my construction
and what is reasoned from it

meaningfulness

meaningfulness
not place
is my fact
as it is to walking
where no absolution is found

using colour

using colour, or on another, for example, complexity
I send messages that are lost in translation
or through filters, scope-morphing when
orientated internally to build possible renditions
or whatever generates meaning in this rich-thinking
are overwritten because through us
sensation is deliciously affecting

away from the figurative
(22nd August 2023)

away from the figurative
memories—whatever or can—
feel very different remembered when others
particularly those that will not be fixed
or correspond necessarily
and have, when
within specific manifestations of sound or paint
more radical differences
can be or in some condition
as a living artwork
comprise of sensations
my body describes as resonance

along the way

along the way
thoughts and happenings
show reality as a perspective
for it's not the same
and I'm not the same
to those as they, when approached
don't elicit a consistent response
experience, memory or meaning
but at each time
only change

presence is where?

presence is where?
when conditions
—embodied and observed multiple conditions—
point to the unseen and disembodied
or with them
when without presence
hold phenomenon as possibility
in now, past or future time

is this state both
or its superposition suited to when
even though its entanglement exists
as one here and there
preparation for becoming simultaneously contingent
only upon looking or measuring
or perhaps even just thinking
to manifest as reality?

alternatively
(23rd August 2023)

alternatively, a degree of obfuscation
generates a similar indeterminacy
where sound shapes outcomes within a moving architecture
and transformation forces a measure of greater delicacy
or not
either to build relationships
or, in the constant that sits within its formations
contort them
are then moulded in greater relational flux
forged through rendition and perception
into a vibration of such intensity
where the violence amplified, distorted, speeded and blurred
particularly where across yet using different
but in any case
to disintegrate or break
that so much pulling here and there smears its detail
from one to another
until eventually, performance closes it
folding the continuum of comprehension
somewhere in time
to manifest as music

words

words, processes of words, word-painting
wilfully describing and analysing shape-territories
opening to those areas surrounding
and through forming the borders of their objects
I script to locate time
which is illusive, obscured
and vague or maybe missing

within texts

within texts
thoughts, sonic memories and words
I words with concept words
and those of landscape and form
become unstable

it troubles me
for when writing, *I am*
in words
as inward thoughts and memories
they mean something inherent in communication
that contradicts a textual resolution and is unsatisfying
knowing full well that when read
all meaningfulness is particular
and may not be transmitted intact
to anyone else

a torrent of stimulation
(24th August 2023)

a torrent of stimulation received, patterned and perceived
brain-charged through to a predictive meaningfulness
challenged only by the unanticipated and the by and by
and as a matter of biology and evolution
is rarely comprehended as a fiction or hallucination
showing I am duped yet fully complicit
in building a convincing simulation

is this why, regardless of contradictory brain fodder
instability as material existence is challenging to embrace
where nature is always inadequately expressed as flux
because word clues attempt to stabilise conditionality
and being immersed in a reliable fantasy
is more compelling than an uncomfortable truth?

filtering out the noise

filtering out noise clarifies the signal
favouring the foreground
as reduction is a natural recourse
of primordial programming

in privileging survival
we hold only a fragment of what is received
there is no embracing the unfiltered enormity of chaos
as the avalanche of incoming data would crush us

accordingly, much passes by unnoticed
and living is experienced through a self-limiting
self-programming, style-generating haze
a half-awareness

artists, less prone to compression
or the paralysis of sensory bombardment, craving more
wish to be overwhelmed
consumed through paint, colour, sound, movement
word, noise and flux

at least I do

and there are others like me
sensation junkies
with no desire for simulacra
for homogenisation, mimesis or anaesthesia
who seek expansion to experience what lies beyond
and to embody those encounters by making

apparently

apparently, physicists make up theories
so that the maths works out

is this why
expressed in words for lay-users
quantum mechanics sounds implausible
transduced from its field of observations, numbers
and symbols?

needs must as science unfolds
and each theory is explained to the popular imagination
but repackaged through an incommensurate symbolic form
is diminished or expanded into other plateaus
perhaps paradox to intimacy, even warmth
bite-sized, embracing the metaphysics of presence

those ideas

those ideas are not permanence
or an offering promising eternal stability
qualifying as truth
they are just glimpses behind the curtain
that find no monkey working the machine
and behind that
another curtain and another
all the way down
into a perpetual falling
where each reveal shows sameness
and reduction
a mind-numbingly claustrophobic compression
and desperation
pushing me to break out
tear down the curtains
and explode this nihilistic pit
into atomised flux and life and light and music
that coalesces as a brighter, expansive view
no more truthful than the former

numbers

numbers are singularities
and physics, their entanglement
waiting to be observed
and again disrupted

being here looking
(26th August 2023)

being here looking, sensing and connecting
tracing a way by eye
and feeling to walk, discover and locate
the term mapping, with its cartographical implications
is appropriate

a relational condition undertaken as body, through body
and how those actions shape what follows
within total immersion
interpreting and responding to inner worlds
their relationship with each other and the land

this lays far for those who
and how first
from experience articulated as thought
territories are assembled from familiar, unfamiliar
and imagined places here and then and there
unwrapped and savoured to make work
forging a singular undertaking as music, painting or writing
embodying how landscape lies at the heart of this experience
and all else passes through it

Bishopstone Folly

yet another relates to a sense of weather
to jeopardy, vulnerability and exposure
and far away
observing changing perspectives
interpreting unpredictable, volatile signs
and as the land and my presence on its surface
oscillates affectively between anodyne and threatening
I calculate my odds

being the tallest object in an open terrain
shelterless
with lightning and thunder
the inevitable drenching
tingling by static charge
and the weight of the sky pushing down
still falling
there is no point in running

Lammy Down

an impression of landscape is related to scale
when distance points a reference between fields, trees
the horizon and
sensing vistas, large across, and height
sky undulations
magnificent and singular as cloudscapes
scaffolding, three-dimensional, expansive and open
distributing the scuttled light and shadow of interplay
across the land
to colour tonal plateaus
as away and ways
of following the sudden appearance of things
illuminating this green, that brown, more and white
moment by moment
when everywhere is transition, instability
and progress to structure and to de-structure
where relationship and significance
only fleetingly register perception as being
in time and place
when sensing a far-flung periphery

Long Covert
(27th August 2023)

change cycles dynamically through time
simultaneously continual everywhere
between light, night, shadow and flowers and seasons
patterning weather and tide
mountains such and rise in physical form when just apart
and deep over temperature
and across millennia that pass by day to day unnoticed
until, as a distant consequence here
seen-surfaces, cliffs, paths, fields and trees disappear

it jars a double-take
first disorientating, then saddening, and finally
its loss equates dissonance in my body
to the considerable effort needed to realign what is
with what was

this is a hinterland of incremental absence
a coastline whose features vanish as they fall into the sea
that over, and now, time prepared
hold no long note of presence
but sound of crumbling, washing away, dissolution
and of fragility

I call this music anxiety
a flow of tiny deaths
that pass into closer time, past time
sea-time
and memory
over and again, submerging
absorbing
to become ghost places

Eastern Bavents

times away
in the warm, sandy lands
bordering low-lying at and by the sea
surge sufficiently to transform intensities
and obsessions that
invested with change and remembering
become multivalent locations
driving further observations of revealing and erosion
that appear through time and
by Suffolk seas, risings and storms

the threat is imminent, but
in mapping or recalling coastal landscapes
owing to wind, waves, depositions
and between relationships of cliff, beach and sky
disappearance to something else can be perceived
but perhaps only as further into the sea

but in holding it
(29th August 2023)

but in holding it
a separation occurs
where the genesis of painting and composing
move from thought and sensation to physicality
external and singular
to be experienced
as new material territories
born from contingency

taken together

taken together
those existing beyond and despite me
or existing inside and because of me
and things I've made that were once part of me
mingle and dance
as lands without borders through which I walk, run, stumble
and play
or am sometimes lost

maps, on the other hand
their materiality implied
are reconstituted through memory
and form my imagined landscapes

holding no certainties
they often mislead

taken apart

taken apart
impressions of elsewhere
offer nothing to hold
and are unreliable

brought together here
the images become stable
drawn by converging lines
and the gravity of half-formed impressions
to where shadows pull at the edges of reason

seeing these familiar snapshots
I exhale
and unfold to open
rooted, yet reaching out
through heartfelt folds and creases

but as every caress falls from my skin
and surprised by what I feel
quickly crumple to close
wondering why any of this should matter
or how any of it could not

presence in knowing

presence in knowing
in something
knowing in absence
to there
emerging from its form
as what is heard
or those not sounded
that sculpt music
when every possible sounded sound there is
every possible signification in time
is produced at once
would I hear to see nothing
and nothing as such density in stasis
neutralises everything
to render music silent
or as the dense monoriot of white noise?

unpredictable and often unstable
(1st September 2023)

unpredictable and often unstable
directed by and through the body
walking as performance is my response to place

it is a dance
a part intentioned, part beyond awareness choreography
a physiology that correlates sensing to movement
giving my work context and structure
tying it to this land
and in free-form
to the body that makes it

like flotsam and jetsam
(11th September 2023)

like flotsam and jetsam
we can be washed to new shores for discovery
or become trapped in eddies that rotate to generate scum

as similar matter
the capacity to float is essential for movement
but progress, journey and value
far from arbitrary
are determined through tide and current
as all points of flow-entry predetermine a destination

perceived as junk or jewellery
privilege shapes our context

such inevitability is tiresome
and with no great hand or storms to shake things up
the drifts and what they carry remain constant

in an age without curiosity

in an age without curiosity
appropriation passes as originality
and aping surfaces, backstory, style and identity
trumps material and intellectual substance
in the stampede for a slice of the dream
for kudos, clicks and fans
and the race to the moral high ground
to build our shiny, brave new world
where truth is marketing
fact is opinion
and everything flourishes
in effortless, epic, brilliant genius

and now

and now, secure in the knowledge of our creator-godness
we shout loudly, declaring the zeitgeist
and its squeaky-clean seen to be lived directives
where through the joys of our virtue, we rise
high in this new democracy
proclaiming other views as subversive and harmful
and protecting ourselves from anything disruptive
retreat to safe spaces for self-care
to never question out loud
for fear of being cancelled

but with little to challenge

but with little to challenge our concepts
we become brittle
and embrace the proximity of this world
omnipotent in our self-congratulatory isolated domains
we surrender the power to choose
or even think for ourselves

assured our opinions are fact

assured our opinions are fact
and that this myopia is truth
we measure value as demand, trend and price tag

while drowning in mediocrity
and by popular demand
judge, jury and executioner are aligned
to suffocate all other expressions until there is nothing
but the relevant, warm embrace of market forces
to justify the quality of our lives

in tending ideas
(14th September 2023)

in tending ideas
if there is nothing to see
here or there
I will shape emptiness to nourish imagination
so that music emerges
in which everything is seen
and everything with density in motion
amplifies itself to endless hearing

smears intensify folding

smears intensify folding in architecture
distorting relationships somewhere formations vibrate
and forces particularly transform shape
either in sound or light to opening out
and away from a continuum identical to slowness
especially misunderstanding
where obscurity broadens confusion, discontinuity
and diminishes resolution and certainty

eventually, this constitution disintegrates
to everywhere pushing
quivering in hyperactivity
while clarity, and from clarity
revelation and construction
pulls performance from sensation
to create something new
and material

Benacre Broad

accumulations of forgotten time
propel shorelines toward entropy
and their hinterlands to neglect

nevertheless, when sparingly experienced
and divested of movement
as out between that pebble-sand landscape
and vanished moments
those shores can be recognised
bordering into something else
while simultaneously ebbing away

here, discord quiet

here, discord-quiet
through disembodiment, ignored and in stasis
where thought disengages a visual-like mediocrity
and gazing misplaces the maelstrom from sound
why not move towards others
where despair vanishes from and around
like an expansion or blur?

neglecting desolate calmness or numbing silence
as a means of embracing nowhere in particular
is a rejection
revealing only its destruction and what is irrational about it
as running wildly to where condemnation is lost
to seek comfort in the meaninglessness of transient realms
becomes a surrender to fiction
from where there is no return

is stagnation pervasive?

is stagnation pervasive
if instant by instant
black, less, and yellow
this dulling of non-things
of gradual disappearance
leading to similarities and towards here
as discordant silence
discordant chaos
apart and disconnection chaos
dissonant
and as a disorder of isolation
shows itself as so insignificant
that when perpetually disregarded
a washed-out existence raises negligence to an art form
that strangles all hope?

when writing to displace
(15th September 2023)

when writing to displace
as a type of movement or detachment that evades emptiness
where in awareness
through filled, noisy remembrances
I speak without quiet voices
as they signify everything external in connection
encouraging a visual assumption that frustrates me
fully understanding that once acknowledged
all purposefulness is thwarted

silent forgetfulness

silent forgetfulness and gibberish
are just empty sounds
for over there
they signify nothing extrinsic in isolation
but brought together here
support an aural confusion
that does satisfy me
because instability is the flow
that dances through comprehension

when opening

when opening my silence in these spaces
to dismantle the edges of identity
I wipe away or lose myself to something else
where walking this borderless land
becomes my comfort and companion

all fragments

all fragments show their displacement once scattered
yet despite this, a portion of the image remains sharp
and now and then, with little present
closing towards the previous
and without scrutiny
many of the parts demonstrate new agreements
and are consistently rigid
showing their completion as fullness

in truth, most are lost
and lucidity
which reveals assurance in narrowing its withdrawal
becomes like smoke and mirrors
so that another understanding is made
and reality developed

found and fulfilled

found and fulfilled
I move away
to empty this abundance
under earth, matter and sky
that once returned
brings it closer
to a natural unity

collected lines

collected lines painstakingly placed together
confines their mode of activity to conceal dissolution
it is something you appreciate
where noise is essential
within knowledge and its embodiment
creating fullness as a strengthening property
it encourages clamour, complexity, roughness and harmony
and one's nature, uniting
advancing through
and how outside, unexpectedly
has ascended a joining
correlating feeling to movement
and thought to matter

it isn't

it isn't that you dislike being misplaced outside the image
as it operates with rigid apathy and resistance

it isn't that you mumble them
into hazy dimensions of numbness

but as a debilitating weakness, you suppress
silence, monotony, smoothness and disarray
and in your mind, dividing out
retreat through deep spaces
and why within, expectedly
descends into a separation
divorcing emotion from making
where before
consistent nothingness
always found resolution as something
to reveal its form

down like a window

down like a window
and surprised by what we hide
such incomprehension becomes vague
contaminated falsehood
and rejecting this, we destroy it from the inside
like so much assimilation and repulsion we find
to then build ruin upon decline

there, illusion constructs ignorance and the surreal
so that expulsion and attraction
pattern them into incompetence

so up like a ceiling
and satisfied by what we reveal
delusion becomes clear, pure authenticity
and embracing that
we bring from it creations
so we might hide from the form of an angel

from a constant viewpoint

from a constant viewpoint
beneath the sky's mass
where the buoyancy of the earth
compresses time into light
I hear sensation expand further into awayness

now open to breath
there is reason to stay

sometimes, I pause
(16th September 2023)

sometimes, I pause before misconception
to apprehend things that aren't what they seem

being unpredictable and sporadically uneven
as the fear of misjudgment is everything
a complete overwhelming fully beneath disorientation
evolves as an anatomy
that encourages dampening and languor
to remain hidden in plain sight
but within the expanse of luminescence and abstractions
lies the familiar texture of pandemonium
where I wait to emerge newly harmonised
but instead, in this pregnant storm of density and noise
shaken up, encounter far more than anticipated
and run with it till exhausted

wavering to the hush

wavering to the hush or unrest inside
or striding out to probe the land
I dismiss equilibrium as a misrepresentation
that shapes what is seen and heard
as places of brightness and theories

this is not an end in itself

this is not an end in itself
or a wholly unfamiliar condition
entirely lost beneath shrouded pulsations that rise to subside
but as emergence within understanding
is never filtered through cool detachment
but is from here rather than from there
a distorted view

in encompassing disarrayed lands

in encompassing disarrayed lands
and far-off prospects
a scene is set
where specifying certainty is never nurturing
but when opened out and conveyed as sound
simulates the separation of self
to here and there simultaneously
to become joyous as music

although much is lost

although much is lost with a noisy brain
it is less than with those
who unplug their minds
to make art that descends into lifeless mimicry

the soundscape dissolves

the soundscape dissolves
through the indifferent ciphering of apathy
erased with blunt strokes
and imprisoned
where music stagnates into paralysis
and blandness infinitely contracts
into a comfortable pit called mediocrity

sometimes steadfastly

sometimes, steadfastly, I resist this blandity
ignoring all presented as minimised
or whitewashed
by those hiding within their smoothing tropes
a neglect of creation's enormity
a lazy undertaking
concealing death by reduction
that stifles any sense of purpose
to recognise, scatter, confound
and reformat experience
as unadulterated, beautiful complexity

it might hinder
(17th September 2023)

it might hinder answers
or guide misconceptions and retorts
but from the dialects of commotion
vivid forms of imagery emerge
as mark is made as word in paint to sound
and zeal in approaching this task emanates from the belief
those explanations of a constructive refrain, verse or chorus
resonate with many
immersed in solitary yet colourful dynamism
where thriving solely on their bright compositions
representation through the forms of quietness
gesture or collapse
remain familiar

and towards the language

and towards the language of imagination
concerning how they embrace their performances
spoken or sung through tongues of clarity and shifting
this discourse is an enlightenment to amplify and vitalise

divorced from the accelerating vacua of prose
it also seeks to radiate out
if there is a method to intensify the fusion
when any indifference to avoiding this task dwindles
to a trivial disconnection of witherings

nevertheless
(18th September 2023)

nevertheless, focusing on their bland designs
and revealed through the patterns of toil
where hidden throughout monochromatic territories
faded shapes of gloom and darkness loom
making any inclusion a misleading coincidence

this encourages stale viewpoints
voiceless compositions and vacuity
as the usual sources of misinformation about their diligence
stretch far beyond my partial involvement
into the responses I conceal in my work

accordingly, I foster an agreement with myself
and retreat entirely from theirs
because distilling that motivation into conversation
is an act to enhance and energise their indifference
regarding how and why
they wholeheartedly embrace their artistry
and condemn all others out of hand

this is what I want to write
(19th September 2023)

this is what I want to write
but I don't know how
or if writing what I want
means what I want it to
or perhaps, hingeing upon how I read words
and what I think they meant when I thought them
they will mean what I want them to mean
when I read them again
or they're read by another

being unlikely, I write implying this, that or many things
from hour to day
knowing precisely what I want words to mean
and just how I want to write them
but fleetingly
as immanent meaningfulness
to express everything necessary
or nothing so much
with particular acuity
and the lightest touch

it's difficult to know
(20th September 2023)

it's difficult to know how to describe them
pulsations, fragmentations, drones
cloud-like densities or vibrating chords
all internally felt-sounds
arising as an immanent response to the downland I walk

they are not yet music
I do not hear them

born of flesh, bone and brain
such corporal noises are unfamiliar
disorganised, drifting through
aperiodic, involuntary and elusive
sensed in my torso, spine and limbs
where I linger in their time-space
absorbed as they course through me

here, the body itself composes
through a union of sensing to performing
without a score, forethought or orchestra
and is primal
being the sonic foundation through which this music flows

at lavender time (Eastern Bavents)

at lavender time
unable to escape the creeping surge
and submerged as the land crumbles
things change
and memories easily fade
into the delightful melancholy of this place

when the fullness
(28th September 2023)

when the fullness of uproar and sense of craving
dilutes in this unreal quiet
cacophony will have synchronised to dull composure
and my light would have dimmed

eventually flooded

eventually flooded with noise, music and utterances
this muteness is dismantled away by loud thinking
its sound puncturing the silence
and while unfolding and still unheard, I take my leave
believing that finally, I get it
only to admire the nuances of my misunderstanding
as I walk away

Knockholt

against the white stuff
secretively under quiet
my back pressed to and hard
and gazing down, then up and around
body plugged into the ground
a current pulses through
holding the earth spin in my gut
as the sky cascades to weightlessness
and gently, in an instant
I move away

these mouths

these mouths aren't vocalising this quietness
so I wonder, doesn't my sensuous loudness
from that universal
from everybody's scream
the primal roar
last only until they hush me
and through exhaustion
execute something merely as a folly
that translocates through acknowledged loss
to compensate with bright tranquillity?

urging correlation

urging correlation between the sensed
and the sound of the sensed
sight is also an embodied element of this compositional act
that, like all its organs of making, echo uniqueness
yet
untouched by another
products of thought remain phantoms
a resonance in silence
a flicker of bright
or flare of sound, reverberating
all boundless in their thoroughfares
and as swift as whispers or light
that despite their brilliance
are formed in this headspace of noise and dispersion
witnessed only by me

what is invisible

what is invisible doesn't numb me
it penetrates as source and purpose in its want
empowering somatics to overwhelm seeing
with the hidden and dislocated
amplifying its vibration
that together enable embodiment of this land
as resonance

around in bustling scenarios
(29th September 2023)

around in bustling scenarios
the radiant, the divulged
are what stimulate outside
where invigoration thrives
especially in complexity
disorder or tactile and bodily forms
as a binary to calm smoothness
that seeks to homogenise all

accepting guidance

accepting guidance through an illuminated conformity
or the sacred mysteries
is impossible
because their core is never disclosed
but only deferred elsewhere
with none of that answering why
the dissonance between my unheard thoughts
and the aspect-juxtaposition to forge a living music
cherishes this entity
through touch and movement alone

here's the latest

here's the latest political expediency
laid on by gatekeepers
who say to lie back, enjoy the ride
and swallow this pre-masticated masterwork

but with nothing to get my teeth into
there's no need to chew
as it slips down a treat
soothing through, over easy

I won't be corralled

I won't be corralled toward tepid confection
the dazzling, the fluffy
nor buy into hype
or play the relevance game
because the trendy choice-makers choices are made
leaving me nowhere to listen
but where they want me to hear

leaving here

leaving here, it inverts to dissipate in the gaps
with a noisy, fleeting separation
and in the commotion, an imperfect structure
a valley where light has departed for the lands of fullness
is formed

no matter, I shall not get lost in its darkness
having loud hopes and imaginings
to illuminate knowledge from opaque nightmares
transforming them into a complex fusion
that through their localised catastrophes
mask my inevitable, utter demise

I imagine

I imagine the expanse is a lacking
perhaps a destroyed mute form
a sprawling, gaping chasm of emptiness
constituting a vacuum that eats light

on another day
maybe a vast, perpetually expanding complex vocal shape
an abundance of sonic possibility
pulsing out rhythm, time, noise and anti-matter
that generates scorching luminescence
within an endless scream

either way
with a displaced listener's sensory collapse
phantasies of absence or presence, scream or silence
or perhaps something else entirely
they fall to empty the abyss of its demons

looking toward
(30th September 2023)

looking toward any horizon earths me
but as physicality holds tight
my mind flies, reaching to feel beyond the boundary of sight
to be pulled there and back here and over again
grasping to comprehend what lies between
that isn't seen

painting requires

painting requires a recalibration
from remembered feelings
to set moments in form through mark-making
and render in-betweenness material
as a Sisyphean task

interpretation is a superpower

interpretation is a superpower
stimulated by what is encountered
moving us towards unfolding
and expression through body, sound, paint and word

even so
we orientate ourselves and move
like intrepid explorers scripting realities
to map what is found
establishing routes across land, fire and water
beneath familiar air
where light bleeding, waxing and waning
illuminates themes and forms
often clearly defined
but also jumbled across a canvas of wildly diverse variants
where the mechanics of life and death cycle through
smearing as they merge
offering confirmation
to enhance our particular view

in aligning ourselves with what we think we know
see, touch and hear
what we believe we are
and what we hope to achieve
it remains presumptuous, dangerous even
to project beyond that threshold
to abandon similitude
advance into unfamiliar, unforeseen territories
and create what is not yet known
as the fact of raucous, confident art

because

because no painting is the land
and no interpretation is the painting
and no single way a monopoly on seeing
there is freedom to express
however necessity shapes me

despite silence's role
(2nd October 2023)

despite silence's role in defining structure
minimising sensory noise is a no-go
as eradicating cacophony's coarser entities
leaves little to work with

finessing and transforming materials
to attain temporal momentum
involves structuring aural and visual-isations in some vague
or clear capacities
to manifest sound-landscapes forged from clamour
or in paint, which also sings

in assembling their dynamically contrasting interiors
a narrative emerges that forms new singularities
as high-resolution consequences of interpretation
expanding meaningfulness exponentially

all representation is amplified

all representation is amplified
when seen silences are dissolved into unmusical instabilities
that once released from limiting spectra
burgeon with possibility

when these quietudes are opened to light
and further disassembled into coherencies
they invert to bright imagery
a treasure trove of potentialities
that, like stem cells, can differentiate
expressed equally as music, painting and more
transforming thought to materiality
and interpretation into a gesamtkunstwerk
they are the threads that connect each form to the other
and all of them to me

there was a passing of whispers
(4th October 2023)

there was a passing of whispers
an exchange of dream-secrets
describing echoes and enigmas resonating from canvas
and in music and words
intimating that to unfold puzzles
one must never surrender to frenzy
as the conscious self liberates
exuberantly awaiting the disclosure of revelations
but listen where the mind holds quiet
to doubts that restrain certainty
generating further questions
or deconstructions preventing superficial interpretations
or stagnation
leading to low-resolution outcomes

obscure moments

obscure moments are exhilarating
when impressions flow freely
enriched by responsive actions that introduce complexity
they conjure intricate scenes within networks of imagination
amplifying the senses

acting accordingly
and secure in my practice
cascades of colour and sound proceed
transcending the surface of my work as a sensual materiality

as each moment arises from process
those unforeseen configurations offer potential
seized, honed and claimed
unifying the fragmented into a whole

once completed, they are set aside for the next
but over time, being unstable
invite revision
becoming forever unfinished
and subject to change

a bridge between

a bridge between what was made
and that being made
leaves an imprint
a history of intention and action
where mapping ever-changing processes thickens it
into a textural palimpsest where colours tangle and negate
that born from this disorder
expand and differentiate elsewhere
into thought made visible

this is a fat surface
(5th October 2023)

this is a fat surface
where energy-fuelled vision thrives
infusing continuity
as traces that comprise skin

sometimes beautiful

sometimes beautiful
always indispensable
and displaying complexities
that are more than once shifting

in intervals of attention
(9th October 2023)

in intervals of attention
wide-open skies lose their significance
and with eyes peeled
a familiar perspective is abandoned
as comprehension coalesces in this opening
to embrace change
but in the jumble of an inner, far-removed place
a maybe, eluding, leading to the everyday
an understanding grows
that the collapse of each painting
rests in my hands
with decisions abandoned
still morphing into unexpectedness
because each brushstroke brings insight
erratic mark-making and raucous colours
showing meaning evaporation within fractured intervals
when they transform
to untold as other awareness

this maze garden
(10th October 2023)

this maze garden
holds a backwards path
leading to the end of summer light
that as I flee, stabilising nowhere
is perhaps a correct progression
like a passing storm before skies clear
or disentangled acuity
or growth
revealed after back-pruning the dead

what banalities

what banalities, then
stagnate from one canvas to another
exposed and unchanged along the way
to embrace or dare blend
hues once and shades
making a distinct solitude
that, in their evolving
now merge our hands in play
beyond a weaving
letting the dark, light
the shadows
where bold dance whispers with luminous dreams
to mark their finds as formless
and inconsequential

revisited

revisited, eventually reworked
and beaten into submission
a new form arises from their wounds
enriched
as struggle is subsumed into technique

diverse remains unfold

diverse remains unfold
like a unity connection or a delicate surface
where scattered elements question simplicity
their layers straddling existence
to perpetually eschew meaning

it is a tapestry combining a hidden core
intricate, embracing odyssey and discord
within a multiplicity, spinning
its convergence unfolding

if I cut it
it generates more and different
each with its own identity
undiminished and new

naughty corner

I have a naughty corner
for those who misbehave
the delinquent
the ones that matter
where pain is growth
and every day, it hurts

not being good
(11th October 2023)

not being good at maths
sometimes, divergent components
—much like these scattered pebbles—
are reluctant to form a coherent image
and won't add up
but watching the sea move among them
my imagination shapes a precise choreography
intricately rendered as sound
smoothly interlocking possibilities
that mirror bodily elegance
as horizons of pulsation and swirls
dance under air laced with gulls
crying out disgorged calculations
that unfortunately
are of no help to me

this consistency in uniting is damaged

this consistency in uniting is damaged
and the viewer remains unaware
lost in ambiguity and uncertainty
it defies description
because when anticipating transparent answers
evasion leads to their abandonment

the beholder's eye

the beholder's eye knows its beauty best
but when this quality is cut, split, fractured or haemorrhaged
individual elements transformed by separation
become several of a once coherent whole
each uniquely so

scattered
they reflect their source
within a lost, now jagged or elastic bonding
that may generate another aesthetic
ever-changing
through the harmony
or disharmony of its forms
the sum of the parts
where multiplying meaning exponentially
into a bonanza of riches
amplifies the artist's capacity
to repurpose, regenerate and recreate anew

should wholeness?

should wholeness
notion traditional unity
when fragmentation
generates multiplicities?

meanings are embedded

meanings are embedded
meanings and execution
and where a work of interpretation is resolved
can, through process
embody a subject as style
with mark-making as meaning-making
mannerism and vision
to discover anew
a different execution and interpretation
as boundaries of paint
reflecting a physicality
where seeing brings a discovered performance
that combines to construct an art object

looking shouldn't numb me
(12th October 2023)

looking shouldn't numb me
not on a Monday
but aren't isolated deviations misinterpretations
or perhaps just other ways of doing or being?

Tuesday isn't unsettled
but if I confuse misconstrued purpose for disfavour
Wednesday's inconsequential conclusions will nevertheless
remain meaningful
and by Thursday, with an erroneous beginning
a derailment perhaps
or bewilderment, entangled and restrained
I cease production as hushed disorders conceal stupidity
that elaborate an inverse design as a way forward

this leads to Friday's disapproval that shows a near collapse
destabilising every place I run to
so that by the weekend
I obliterate canvases as an act of renewal
only to find it's Monday again

establishing unstable brushwork

establishing unstable brushwork
prevents me from cloning the scene
but ever questioning
I stretch visual relationships
to yield familiar concepts
scrutinise old orientations
and authenticate others
causing their actions to multiply
within fertile uncertainties

when reviewing what is made

when reviewing what is made
image homogenisation becomes a nonsensical strategy
a safety net
pulling my centre toward conformity
but then, always moving away
I establish a divergent materiality through play
that speaks of another seeing
and a bravery beyond now

to be good enough
(14th October 2023)

to be good enough
loved, accepted, in demand
spinning around the world like being with success
and bound tightly to identity
as addiction and compulsion
all dreams are cast
but so often atrophy
as life plays out

fleeting hope

fleeting hope weighs dense
as an involuntary music of sinking
it creeps out to dwell in between breath
and is often overlooked when confronted by the stark reality
of others' worth, status and success
as their echoing self-endorsed eulogies and proclamations
stick in the mind long after the event
cutting deep to fester

jealousy looms

jealousy looms when another's fortune is favoured
and judged as worthy or not against deserving
so that angry and rebellious
aching vulnerability may shine
relentlessly fuelling anxiety
while waiting with bated breath for the nod and favour
—to be seen, wanted and admired—
becomes the saddest life-long vocation

chasing dreams

chasing dreams
believing that while present
there's still time
hopeful for the spotlight to fall on me
nevertheless knowing that if it does
it will quickly divert to another
bringing back the shade
that heralds a return
to the gloomy suburbs of life

who am I kidding?
(15th October 2023)

who am I kidding?
if I were indifferent, it wouldn't hurt
this isn't a neutral response
it is a falling in the pit of my stomach each time I think it
a stranglehold that wrings me dry
but still, I wait
still, I want it
just a sign, a whisper, a glimmer of hope

but in, over and with

but in, over and with my particular sense of beauty
powering up opportunities that migrate towards frustration
sharpens my defiance
to fuel actions as a necessary act
solely about the assembly
and about invention, the clarity
the tangible proof of the thing itself
to claim these paintings and music as my resistance
and my resilience
each a reminder of paths barred on the journey
but in so doing
pushing towards challenges
towards disappointment
requires a substantial effort to affirm life
and find ways to persist
so each day, I rise as a necessary beginning
self-bolstering
but with many failed attempts at stability
paying attention to noise as a testament to eagerness
my power slowly ebbs away to a place not quite present
but alive enough to feel and care
about this culturally selective mass extinction event
—a mechanics of ugliness in operation—
to oust my kind
and our music
as a celebrated joy of this age

reluctant to perish

reluctant to perish
and when gripped by failed attempts to succeed
I act out explosive scenarios in my head
yelling with such force
spit and snot fly around
as the tangle of pain passes through
turning obstacles into chaos
dulling my destruction, my silence of moments
so I can reassemble their incoherent forms
into colour and sound made art

you'd think I'd be immune

you'd think I'd be immune by now
ground down with no fire in my belly
but because of the rage
and its sublimation to pain
this passion finds no rest
to extinguish its flames

thoughts darken

thoughts darken in the morning glow
overshadowing to eat away
as my brain dances a solitarily, well-worn choreography
a recognition of longing
rather than resilience and patience
as a testament to endless waiting
or to smile
and muster the strength to breathe
because as time moves outwards
and repeating in my head
"they're busy; they're always busy"
and
"perhaps tomorrow"
brings that desperate slither of comfort false hope buys
for a moment or two
each day

a remembered beginning
(16th October 2023)

a remembered beginning
thrives somewhere away from here
initiating distinctness of attraction
with delights resembling whims
where enthusiasm eventually fades
submerging a far-flung joy
distant
and indistinguishable before or behind
after which
comes the loathing

passion often falls short

passion often falls short of arrival
as what once pleased now diverges
to repulsion or ritual
cultivating sameness as toward nowhere
it dwindles
to a well-versed ending

joy drowns despair

joy drowns despair

sometimes

but apathy never outpaces arriving

when attracted to destinations

when attracted to destinations
a solid outflow compresses involvement
it inhibits seeing
or erases what is heard
to misshapen out the lacking
attempting to identify the boundaries
and parcel up, box in and detach
even though time cannot be marked or cut
or shaped into neat bundles of starts and stops
as formless, its flow is motion
where only difference defines the merging

now quiet

now quiet, they veer away
and with fearless egos, blurring their path
tread by desire and louder, voice in their gates
wield their impact through harm wrapped in kindness

with surgical precision
penetrating skin with a smile
their violence leaves no surface trace

this strategic cruelty is an art form
and the wrenching inside
all that is left of its mark

with fullness in music
(17th October 2023)

with fullness in music comes an imponderable
with no beginning
where discordant and erratic relationships
endlessly generate sound
like today, when listening in my mind
two muted trumpets dissolved into none
as music's temporality moved away
becoming further emergence
for this is no finished piece
nor does it start from here
but manifests in transient form when heard or imagined
for as long as I can differentiate its moments
from what it is not
and as it absorbs
back into the unfolding continuum of time
remains forever ephemeral

foolishly

foolishly, I attempt to hold, name and shape it
this helps me find my way
but then, remembering
loosen my grasp and let it move through

sometimes in clarity
(18th October 2023)

sometimes in clarity
listening is liberated
from imagery, tropes and metaphysics
to embody only what is sound
immanent and unknowable
in its time-bending enormity
where imagination and interpretation range
brilliantly significant, moving, deep and personal
when in those moments
everything else is unnecessary
and meaningfulness becomes comprehension

Idstone Down
(22nd October 2023)

the sky folds in behind me
throwing a reddish-dull haze as I stroll
and with each step, exhaling depth and stillness
my closeness to the land magnifies boundaries to sharpness

I love this place
where the surface flattens
revealing shallow billowings of warmer air
now red-orange
the shades that dim and weaken as the day fades
flowing into music composed through walking
in this light, land and time

shaped outside awareness
by my body's interaction with the ground
and my eyes and all senses pulling streams of sound
this way and that
as immanent embodied composition gushing through
with orchestras above, below and within, moving with me
shadowing every form
responsive
their emanation stretching to the horizon and beyond
as a sonic torrent, dense, vital and intricate
one moment cascading into the next

this is my music
and it is strange

noise

noise, this is not your moment
with volumes of quiet that way and this
the world is silent for now
and with each step, inhaling shallowness
until never or an eternity, it leaves
in weightlessness, staying temporarily adrift
but remaining everlasting
where depth elevates concealing
and my ears with no sensations pushing
flare out music decomposed through muting

in brightness

in brightness, standing
with thought held close
directing one moment flowing into the previous
unshaped inside consciousness by imagination
the now blue-green shades brighten and intensify as time
with cool quietudes below, above and outside
diverting away
immediately change to yellow noise

startled, I drop it
shattering the continuum of silence
into fragments of multiscopic sound
resembling music
before its consolidation to orange-red sonority
and the changeability of perception
to a rarely-seen brilliant white light

Hackpen Hill
(1st November 2023)

calming eastwards above the flowers
wandering before symmetry into the stands
deeply connecting amidst the dull white and grey flowing air
the doves converge here above the breeze
high peaceful thoughts, I imagine
and greatly attached to the land
warm, unburdened below-ground
and above
forward motionless standing
amplifying earth soar-under and over up
when, through touch
the sky seems closer down
and gradually, everywhere, my senses expand
as time advances within my seeing
with feelings of attraction to beyond
in the meadows, depths, the hills and all outside my skin
life seen through beauty and ugliness
balances simultaneously a melding of noise and motion
progressing outward beneath stirring
westerly
to the far beech trees

time recedes

time recedes
as a sense of repulsion turns within
and the truth of what lies in the wastelands
of heaven's summits
and the shallows of gravel hills
the woodlands and all inside
shows itself
as a death through decay
glimpsed momentarily
as I fall

Fyfield Down

it's impossible to escape
or scatter in dust and chattering
as sparrows do when disturbed
excited to discover flourishing life
or new vistas

from this labyrinth
where the brilliance of existence, vast and profound
follows its course
I stare outward
entangled
hoping to see where they fly
and be bird just once

All Cannings Down

skylarks shaking and vibrating ever so gently
against the blue, grey-white and sun-sounds
cascade from around above
where hearing their highest, intricate songs
feels safe and deeply warm
while familiarly attached to the ground
moving forwards, sideways, looking up, down
feeling the chalk earth run through me
it pulsates and reconfigures into blazing sound and colour
as my body responds in kind
choreographing a different music not bound to light or air
but on a lazy walk southwards
shaped through movement and time

a familiar atomisation
(2nd November 2023)

a familiar atomisation
dispersing beneath the silence
low, dangerous thoughts
profoundly detached and cool
unburdened below air

imploded yet shifting within a vivid, fiery black language
shadows of discord dissolve unity
to beyond where this body can reach
overwhelming the now into an eternity
too thick to penetrate

of sound and activity

of sound and activity generating life
moving through to coalesce deeply
the grey, white and blue against, vibrating
I reach forwards
looking to see the sounds above the sun
high, safe and magnificent
to what under in the fields, the land crevices
the depths the grass folds
branches and all around
a catalyst with ablaze prose
and vivid-form words
earthing ideas that drive music outward
when thought, written or spoken

at dusk
(7th November 2023)

at dusk
its remaining to forget
the sky reduces borderlines
to gentleness

within release

within release, as time frees through
under a muted sky
and vanishing below its glow
while outside here
others contract
as years anchor through
but sitting on this beach
looking out again
over and over
playing with fine sand dust
cool between my fingers
I'm idly advancing too

it's a simple path
(14th November 2023)

it's a simple path outside the restless soul
but asleep
lost in the confusion of an underworld
wrapped in illogical thoughts
near the intense mind-heat
of dreaming a distorted time-flow
this instability
unremarkable yet singular
wanders a familiar shifting landscape
only to return with a sense of meaningfulness
that colours the day a dull yellow melancholy

asleep

asleep, regressing to the inner world
an audacious imagination finds life in the fury
where nearby earth agitates
and I act out
but enslaved to the body
cannot wander far

the notion of celestial realms

the notion of celestial realms
governing the disarray of the cosmos
its complexities and immensity are convenient
but ignores this engulfing numbness
to repel the obvious
as my eyes and ears are neither here
nor there in the distance

but within, there's a harmonious noise
perhaps whispering or beckoning, pulling forwards
but with no destination given beyond wishful thinking
it is likely imagination feeds insecurity
guiding toward warmth, hope
and a desired comprehension of this vastness

if dullness is the silence of sleep

if dullness is the silence of sleep
sleep, the silence of unawareness
unawareness, the silence of numbness
numbness, the silence of nonexistence
and nonexistence itself silence
what, then, is nonexistence
and how would I be numb to realising I'm engulfed in it
when sounds themselves are unsure of their shadows
and shadows whisper of blank depths
what, then, are these depths
and how do I close them away?

and when searching and peering through
how do I stop canvases from questioning their colours
or their forms when looking on
as interpretation constructs endless possibilities
like the introspection of music
where quiet existence is itself
a labyrinth for unseen murmurs to flow?

what, then, is their essence?
are they an abundance, like completion through emptiness
and how do I fill those labyrinths of absence
as they reach out ever into infinity
to the very beginning of utterance
or those lazar-like glimpses
cutting through me
as my eyes, heavy, drowning under imagery
see light fall like dust from my hands onto the floor
dispersing into a wild tapestry of borders, hinterlands
and abstractions
opening onto another chaotic world?

not directly touched

not directly touched
my music remains a trace
a resonance in silence
where introspection
barely registers its shape beyond evaporation

but on expansive days
being moved
this residue becomes a reverberant tapestry
expanding
as each moment directly amplifies to sound
and I find something within its vast uncharted space
where, as a fleeting, ephemeral voice
—an unknowingness
a touched silence and free confusion of dissonance—
I feel the bluntness of meaningful spaces
as a focused, harsh reality
where through covert ignorance
truth builds to a temporal creation
making an assembled disorder

here, art whispers sharpness
and soothes with a closeness, gentle in variable confusion
and if calming
an insignificant realisation may settle this insecurity
fullnessing out the vast quiet moving freely about
towards a point where all music flows
into emptiness

only then
can I find my place within it

as the hushed sky drives me

as the hushed sky drives me slowly toward indifference
the penny drops
that there's no resolution to be found in this place
only a vague haze obscuring the evening's rationality
and while the cool air implies a dulled confusion
where patterns form to then dissolve
any illusion of an early spring is shattered

apathy tranquilises me

apathy tranquilises me backwards
as falling, adrift in time
a sensory shrinking within
coalesces into numbness
and a grey rhythm of uncertainty prevails
to birth anarchy that consumes equilibrium
and widen the chasm

turbulent hues paint twilight
(16h November 2023)

turbulent hues paint twilight as a rebellious tranquillity
a foreboding even
when warmth retreats
to night unravelling across the fields
and in those dark, cold places
irrationality triumphs
revealing the primitive within

a grey solitude
(Rafford, 1st January 2024)

a grey solitude stretching whispers into cadence
through terrains of forgotten names
washed clean and smooth by the tide
a transcendent unfixing of truth
smelling wet, cold sand
and a clarity that advances
here, where the breeze and immanent silence
huddle and listen
as subdued by drowned echoes
wandering the wastelands, none
not one is remembered or marked
or made grit by biting easterlies or gulls' cries
not one pierces the skeletal silence of waning days
that accentuate emptiness across this shoreline
pushing in until my ears throb

only isolation advances lost voices
into the barrens remembered as pulsation
a heavy surge of rhythm
unwavering, relentless, enormous and melancholic
submerged somewhere out to sea
over and ever calling

through languages of obscurity

through languages of obscurity and ignorance
subdued shapes of vagueness emerge
downcasting precise dimensions of feeling
to unravel emptiness as a weakening liability
now disclosed

as the sea shrinks

as the sea shrinks, concealing its contours
pulling away from the familiar
an intense undertow rises back onto the land
where its narration contracts
and my reaction shapes what precedes it

here, a stillness
more resistant than constricting
creates opportunity for the gradual disappearance of things
ambiguous or possibly complete
somewhere outside duration
generating a time-song wailing
a hollow
disembodied and vile

by and through it

by and through it
a lyrical confrontation unfolds
a cacophony of ideas
where sifting through
my account shapes reason

launching into the sea

launching into the sea
in the warm, sandy lands
and embraced by the difference
my story expands

tones of white
(2nd January 2024)

tones of white, crimson, tangerine, gold
purple and more
strewn here and there
into theories crystallised across the sky
streaming, ordinary and marvellous as sunsets
or sunrises
a concealing of physics, refraction and explosive light
immanent
moving through air
where visual dissonances harmonise to break apart
amplifying sounds that reverberate as colour
like a music in my head
whole or possibly duration
outside somewhere else
and beyond reach

this sensation
(Crewkerne, 11th January 2024)

this sensation of suspended time and physicality
engages as vibration and sinking to expand simultaneously
and in my nostrils
a transfixing odour, sometimes metallic
of hyperreality greater than any moment
compels consciousness beyond here to absolute being

disembodied, static, but utterly alive in motion
time suspends
just for a second
until self-awareness kicks in
and bodily connection
causes an instantaneous implosion of mind
yanking me back to earth with a thud
when all is transformed
to confined, dulled, resonant memory

craving to recreate this ecstasy so my work may fly
reaching, grasping for it
is failure

what was immanent collapses
into my here and now
—the observed and observer—
a superdense centre
that immediately reformatted as *this* temporality
fractures into comprehension
and is lost forever

The Wenninger Letters
January-February 2024

marks as signs
(Crewkerne, 12th January 2024)

marks as signs of sound made visible
are traces signifying chimeric music only I can hear
although fixed
their shapes initiate auralisation
that, when listening back or remembering
change within the ebb and flow of life
sometimes radically so
but moreover
what results from another's interpretation
is voiced as something else entirely
moving performance from within
to over there

being sound flowing
(13th January 2024)

being sound flowing as time
always changes me
it leaves a trace beyond immanence
unfolding possibility

a singularity

a singularity
can only be answered
by another of its kind
as shifting and peculiar
its meaningfulness
its truth
is apprehended through something that
no matter its symbolic form
offers a comparable
or different conditionality
to reason with

here, where future and past are sharp-edged
(21st January 2024)

here, where future and past are sharp-edged
experience catapults into splintered realities
each holding possibilities others will want to stabilise
but with self-proclaimed correct renditions
likely scripted falsehoods
all interpretive certainty should be questioned

he says

he says
he plays only what is written
knowing that this is not me or mine
but an invitation that signifies terms of engagement
not to replicate but to iterate
making a novel and rather distinct original
a Heraclitian blueprint
born through reinterpretation
heterogeneous
as our rivers flow
to briefly entwine

negotiating this sonic terrain

negotiating this sonic terrain
a symphony, unorchestrated, raw
and sometimes alien
is a dance of opposites
where beginnings defy conclusions
flourishing through experiences
that merge into a singular plateau
as misinterpretations morph into unscripted realities
strange pathways
that embrace the indistinct
a flux-flow
where creation is not an end but an ongoingness
rushing through
to take my breath away

in the confinement of predictable ground

in the confinement of predictable ground
they produce a clarity filled with clichés
adaptable to every explanation
and mirroring their standards for validation
hold dominion through repetition, affirmation
and ceaseless stagnation

when walking

when walking
perception can be so clear
that a sense of stability is forged
but do not be fooled
this is often a reflection
a revealing of the inner self
appearing solid, separate
two, yet not two
and misleadingly so
when *the other*
is just *the one*
seen from an unfamiliar perspective

the way ahead folds abruptly

the way ahead folds abruptly
imploding into a sketchbook of thoughts
a disordered, illegible and scattered collection
where meaning and its formation
are lost forever among the pages
unable to be conjured back as was
yet still triggering the crafting of a score
that sings a vision
now transformed
into something else entirely

but ignore all that

but ignore all that
in forms so alike
their opacity
an exterior and interior blurring
is predominantly unified
to conceal in illusions
none yet both

thinking upwards

thinking upwards
affirms the sky as a silent canvas
but outside
navigating the free-air
there is much noise
differences abound, so similarities scatter
and within a world unnoticed yet distinctly seen
discord and harmony separate
into black-and-white hearing
as the music of duality emerges

nature is a deferred uniqueness
(22nd January 2024)

nature is a deferred uniqueness
but easily confused with subjectivity
and approached through taste
becomes superficial
and simply depicted
as a sensual composite
or romanticised view

fascinating tenses

fascinating tenses
acknowledge the moment of transition
in a potential composition
where numerous beginnings end
in the same casual scribblings
sowing meanings
that feed an insatiable hunger
to know
but where understanding remains incomplete
scrambled or lost
no matter how many notes are cast

in the fluid expanse

in the fluid expanse where thoughts merge
a powerful transduction of meaningfulness blossoms
resonant and rich
bridging our inner worlds
where signs travel from one to another
in a crucible empowering interpretation
through sound, paint and word

and responding

and responding to what is there
he weaves a violin's line through the breath of a flute
not as rearrangement
but connected to the former
as rebirth into a new plateau of sound
ripe with dense possibility

traces the composer leaves behind

traces the composer leaves behind
are a map of raw potential
morphing seamlessly into sound, into movement
becoming architecture, flavour
a brushstroke across an unseen canvas
or another
as interpretation has it

this is where possibilities stretch unbounded
as perception and creation collide
with sparks flying out
melding transformation
so that meaningfulness is made

this is no imitation

this is no imitation
or the encoding of emotion
it is the catalyst of interpretation
manifested as a shared entity
sculpted by our bodies and minds
a space where the familiar is deconstructed and reborn
in an endless cycle of reimagining
so that understanding is forged through unfolding

if we sketch together
(1st February 2024)

if we sketch together
looking out here
would we make identical drawings
exact replicas of the sea and sky
using our conceivable artistry
just you beside me
or build something different
from the sameness we see?

with precise stance

with precise stance
flute in hands
he plays
and through breath
offers all interpretation
as each note
passing to the next
resonates with our possibilities
now material as sonic flight
cumulative and expanding
it moves towards fullness
in flux
and with each hearing opens

where do they stand?

where do they stand
when claiming, "this is my performance?"
and why is what I hear
more theirs than mine?

when reading scores
(12th February 2024)

when reading scores
a topography of signs and symbols emerges
gateways to uncharted potential
where interpretive space
breathless and dizzying
is the core of creation
for vision and energy to perpetually rejuvenate
here, their implied sounds, once imagined
become a distinct world, continuously evolving
brimming with tangible alchemy
and colour-field imagery

remembering the work I dreamed

remembering the work I dreamed
felt, yearned for and conceived
urges me to craft another
that sings that sound
a thousand different ways
each beguiling in its richness
and ecstatic with sonic torsion

wide over
(14th February 2024)

wide over
dynamic and beyond here
a union forms
converging the stories that bind us
where intimacy tightens across the narrow closeness
and movement again or within
shows our accounts diverge
forming a bond without shape
or kin

we bypass the complexity

we bypass the complexity each message holds
blundering across the expanse that separates us
to where our meaningfulness flows
into a nexus without correspondence
making touch impossible

now stranded
we are the sole witnesses
to a mutually exclusive understanding
that even conceived under a different light
like us
will remain forever distinct and independent

with minds engaged

with minds engaged
we search among the familiar
to navigate layers of complex truth
hoping understanding fosters a truce
that blends narratives as an evolution
guided by gentle consciousness
where our testament to success
is the fantasy of a shared reality

if knowledge is the construct of learning

if knowledge is the construct of learning
learning, the construct of discovering
discovering, the construct of seeking
seeking, the construct of curiosity
and curiosity itself, a construct
what, then, is knowledge
and how would I discover that I possess it?

I tread carefully
(17th February 2024)

I tread carefully
knowing interpretation is a gamble
when matched to intent
and to better understand
often draw on paper
where line as thought
shows patterns words hide

drawing your thoughts

drawing your thoughts as feelings that spin
to catch storms speech cannot hold
emotions, reflections perhaps
of unique noises
from one that moves this freely
among layers constantly revealing
exploring the unsaid, the bound, the profound
in every line intimated
and where discharged, not exposed
the voice opens ideas
to expand everything and release
or just around everyone and everything
as a notion mirrored
or the detonation of sound in my head
no one else can hear

at its core

at its core
these threads unravel the fabric
of creation's fundamental unit
the original or atom
as Democritus would have it
to bind no knowns within the imagination
endlessly amplifying their value

split the object

its significance multiplies infinitely
recognised as an entirety, a singularity
where the potential within emerges
as two immaculate originals
full and potent

is thinking art?

is thinking art
when visions, figments of seeing, of unheard sound
of smell and touch, crafted
residing in dreamscapes uniquely accessible
and mine to visit, play, mould and breathe at will
their plasticity as familiar as the painted or performed
become my ghost music and imagined landscapes
where the merest notion of them
conceived in thought
is art enough
or is it that to be real
art must be made material beyond skin
encounter another's sensing
and be acknowledged as object and entity
outside of me?

230

the feel of it

the feel of it
the perception of being
makes interpretation enough
even when senses are deluded, their wires crossed
a known recurrence
where fact and fiction interlace
as each moment ripples inwards
building a variable reality from experiences
sensation upon sensation flowing through, up and over
so that understanding sweeps change into the air
to embrace the pulse of life in motion
but taken together
what is the truth of it all
when breathing
in the fluidity of time?

uncertain where my feet may fall

uncertain where my feet may fall
and attempting to remain upright
today, I move slowly forward
my eyes fixed hard on the ground

accepting this, I wander in thought
but seldom see around or far enough ahead
to know where I'm bound
or why I should be going there

but then
(19th February 2024)

but then
if there were another
would they merge or diverge when playing in unison
echoing a shared truth
carried by air?

untouched by it

untouched by it
and now at war with everything other
they demonise art
inverting its thesis for being
into a social ill
to be called out, shamed
purged and abandoned

outside summer's shortest day

outside summer's shortest day
my body welcomes a calm sky
its brief harmony
and honeyed, warm sensations
played through as a prelude to battle
where, casting shadows, swell and unyielding
its affray becoming an endless numbness from the fight
it cloaks light and roars
as all is tainted
eclipsed by fire before darkness falls
and life is scattered to the four corners of hopelessness

but in the morning

but in the morning
harmony, calm from its night terrors
—a form of order balanced within the structures of noise
of shaping and misshaping
or light, earth, construction and birth—
is a meticulous dance of elements over and again
reborn into clarity
through the outing of a connection into air
where unbounded, its body embraces a fullness
through synthesis acknowledged as transience
of becoming, of warmth, into moving
a multivalent time convulsion
cascading towards completion
as the immanent condensation point of thought into music
where vibrations made material, transcending flesh
find their place beyond me
to coalesce, trigger and reflect back
as resonance on paper

236

this music is a rapid journey

this music is a rapid journey
its entity, a peculiar precision
particular in its flexibility and mutual invention
made audible through another's hearing
where, as this sonic universe unfolds
altering the fabric of now-time
warping reality—for a while
it casts shadows onto worlds
each uniquely their own
within space
a series of beginnings
interpreted from notation
and contorted by the gravity of this performance
into a body without borders
reaching out

so, I embrace it
(23rd February 2024)

so, I embrace it
my brush dipping into colour
turmoil to canvas—moving
hues blending at the edge of tension
perilously close to black mud
sliding into and out of focus
wondering if awareness will be today's awakening
as every day, where chaos dances
escaping explicit form
of shades clashing without care or resolution
where my alertness and feeling—
as in this abstraction, a landscape of sorts
feeling the outcome of being, of painting—
unfurls
each stroke, a testament to the existence
of its materiality
my physicality
and of certainty in these things
but later, away from all this
how would I *feel* this state of being
to know that I am truly aware of it
other than through myself, over and over
with this as the only proof available
to reason why I'm here?

above all else

above all else
sound is the sensation that gives me awareness
as lucidity of existence
the you, why and how are separate
when wakefulness moves from misunderstanding
to break the noise that becomes being
and of sensation
what now is set apart from it?

Marc Yeats

Poems in alphabetical order

Printed and bound by CPI Group (UK) Ltd, Croydon, CR0 4YY

02/09/2024

01031083-0002